SEP 14 '92 FEB 10 '96   JUL 05 '97 NOV 27 '04
DEC 11 '92 MAR 08 '95   APR 2 1998
            APR 05 1995 APR 28 1998
                         DEC 16 '98
FEB 11 '93 SEP 04 '96   FEB 02 '00
            JAN 16   JUN 02 '99
AUG 18 '93 JUL 22   FEB 17 '00
FEB 10 1994   JUL 16 '00
            OCT 28 '9   AUG 22 '00
JUL -7 '94 DEC 20 1995 SEP 06 '00

MAR 31 '03

PICTURE LIBRARY

GUINEA PIGS

PICTURE LIBRARY
GUINEA PIGS

Norman Barrett

Franklin Watts

New York   London   Sydney   Toronto

©1990 Franklin Watts Ltd

Franklin Watts Inc
387 Park Avenue South
New York
NY 10016

Designed by
Barrett and Weintroub

Photographs by
Marc Henrie
South American Pictures
Pat Morris
Bruce Coleman/Jane Burton
Mary Evans Picture Library

Illustration by
Rhoda and Robert Burns

Technical Consultant
David Alderton

Library of Congress Cataloging-in-Publication Data

Barrett, Norman S.
    Guinea pigs/Norman Barrett; [photographs by Marc Henrie . . . et
al.; illustration by Rhoda & Robert Burns].
        p.   cm.   (Picture library)
    Summary: Examines guinea pigs around the world, describing their
appearance, habitats, feeding and reproductive habits, and life
cycles, and providing tips for their proper care.
    ISBN 0-531-14031-8 (U.S.)
    1. Guinea pigs—Juvenile literature.   2. Guinea pigs as pets—
Juvenile literature.   [1. Guinea pigs.]   I. Henrie, Marc, ill.
II. Burns, Rhoda, ill.   III. Burns, Robert, ill.   IV. Title.
V. Series.
QL737.R634B37   1990
599.32'34—dc20   89-21528
                                                        CIP
                                                        AC

Contents

Introduction

Guinea pigs are among the gentlest and most easily cared for domestic animals. They have been popular family pets for hundreds of years.

They are plump little animals, with a large head, small ears and short legs. Their feet are small in comparison with the rest of their body, and they have no tail.

Wild guinea pigs live in South America. They belong to the cavy or cavia family and this is another name for the guinea pig.

△ A pet guinea pig in what is known as tortoiseshell and white coloring. Many pet guinea pigs, like this one, are of the short-haired type.

Domestic guinea pigs come in a variety of colors and coat types. These range from the long-haired Peruvian, which looks just like a floor mop, to the more familiar short-haired guinea pig.

Guinea pigs are very timid animals. Any sudden noise makes them rush for cover. They enjoy the company of others, and are usually kept in pairs or in families.

△ The long-haired, Peruvian guinea pig is considered by many to be the most beautiful of the pet varieties, even though it sometimes resembles a mop!

Looking at guinea pigs

Wild

The wild Peruvian cavy is the ancestor of all domestic guinea pigs. It has coarse, mottled gray fur. There are many kinds of cavies in the wild. They all live in South America.

Teeth and claws

The teeth and claws of guinea pigs both grow continuously. The powerful incisor teeth are worn down by gnawing.

Incisors

Claws can grow too long and may have to be trimmed with clippers. Guinea pigs have four toes on their front feet and three toes on their hind feet.

Domestic

Domestic guinea pigs are rounder, plumper and heavier than wild cavies. They have been bred with attractive variations in coat type – long-haired, rough-haired and smooth – and in an ever- increasing range of colors.

Making a home for your guinea pig

Guinea pigs dislike the cold and are usually kept indoors. But they can live outdoors in sheltered areas so long as their hutch contains plenty of warm, snug hay for bedding. In good weather, they can use an outdoor run like this "ark," with a cozy, closed-in sleeping area. You may also want to put wire over the base of the ark, so that the guinea pigs cannot escape when their run is moved. Guinea pigs love "toys" that they can gnaw on.

Cavies

There are 14 known species (kinds) of guinea pigs, or cavies, in the wild. These have long, coarse, gray or brown fur, a coloring that is called "agouti."

Guinea pigs are not pigs. They are rodents. In addition to the cavies, there are a number of other closely related species, such as the paca, the degu and the chinchilla.

▽ The cuis, a type of wild guinea pig, has the typical agouti coat of all wild cavies.

The wild ancestors of the guinea pig lived on grassland. Some cavies burrow, or tunnel, but they cannot jump or climb.

Domestic guinea pigs were first bred from wild cavies hundreds of years ago, by the Inca Indians of Peru. But it is not known which species of cavy they came from.

△ A chorus line of degus, close relatives of the cavies. These rodents, unlike the guinea pig species, have tails.

Domestic types

The three main varieties of domestic guinea pigs are the English short-haired, the Abyssinian rough-haired and the Peruvian long-haired.

Of these, the English short-haired, with its fine, glossy coat, is the most common. It is the easiest to breed and to look after.

The most common colors of the English short-hair are white, brown, black and orange, and mixtures of these. Other colors include lilac, chocolate, beige and red.

△A pair of English short-haired guinea pigs, with their smooth, glossy coats.

The Abyssinian, or Abby, breed has a wiry coat of rough hair made up of swirls called "rosettes." They have a ruff, or collar, and a back ridge made up of stiff hairs.

The Abby is a beautiful animal that seems to enjoy bustling about. It is not difficult to care for and is reputed to be among the most intelligent of guinea pigs.

▽ An Abyssinian guinea pig, with its rosette-patterned coat. This is a brindle variety, a mixture of black and orange.

The Peruvian breed, with its long, silky hair, is regarded by many as the most beautiful of all guinea pigs. But it is a little more expensive and is a pet for people with time to spare.

The Peruvian requires regular and careful grooming. Its coat needs combing daily to keep it from matting, and might need a shampoo about once a month.

△ A Peruvian guinea pig, with its long, silky hair almost covering its face. Sometimes it is difficult to tell which end is which with this breed.

Other types of domestic guinea pig include the Sheltie and the Teddy.

The Sheltie, or Silkie, was bred originally from Peruvian breeds. It has the same long, silky hair, but it grows in a different way. It flows back from behind the ears, leaving the head clear.

The Teddy, or Rex, is similar to the Abyssinian. It has rough, kinky hair, but no rosettes.

▽ The Sheltie has long hair that combs backwards, behind its face.

◁A pair of American Teddy guinea pigs, mother (right) and son. Their coats are short and thick, and coarse to the touch. This is a relatively new breed, and is known in Britain as Rex.

Coat coloring

Whatever the type of coat, there are a great number of color varieties and markings, especially in the English short-hairs.

Self-color means that there is just one overall solid color. Agouti coloring means that the tip and base of each hair is dark, with a band of another color in the middle. Other types of coat markings include Dalmatian, Himalayan and tortoiseshell and white.

△ Agouti guinea pigs in three different colors – Silver (left), Gold (the baby) and Lemon. Other Agouti colors include Cinnamon, Salmon and Chocolate.

▷ A Self Chocolate has a rich brown coat.

▽ Not quite white, this is a Saffron Argente, with red eyes.

△Abyssinians also come in different color varieties and markings.

◁The roan is a black guinea pig with white hairs evenly intermixed throughout its body coat.

▷ A tortoiseshell and white guinea pig.

▽ More short-haired color varieties, showing various combinations of markings.

Life of a guinea pig

Most species of wild guinea pig live in groups of 5 to 10, although some dig tunnels and live in large colonies.

Guinea pigs are timid animals and have no defense against enemies except to run away. But they are very alert. They stay in burrows or among rocks during the day, and come out to eat at night. They live on grasses, leaves, grains and fruit.

△ A Silver Agouti guinea pig with her 1-day-old pups. Unlike most other rodents, which are born blind, naked and helpless, the baby guinea pig is fully formed at birth. The newborn pup has its eyes open, a full coat of fur, and can eat solid food. It can run within minutes of birth.

Although they are not pigs, adult female guinea pigs are called sows and males are called boars. But the babies are known as pups.

In the wild, guinea pigs breed twice a year, with only one or two pups in each litter. Domestic guinea pigs have up to four litters, of 2 to 10 pups, each year.

Guinea pigs are fully grown after a year. Wild guinea pigs may survive for 5 or 6 years, domestic breeds for 8 years or more.

▽ A Self Beige sow with her 4-day-old pups. Guinea pig young do not need much care from their mother, who feeds them with milk for three or four weeks. The young guinea pig is itself ready to breed at six months old.

Guinea pigs are known for the range of vocal sounds they can make. They are the most talkative of all the small mammals.

The familiar high-pitched whistle or "wheep" means they want food. Tame guinea pigs "wheep" when they hear a refrigerator opened!

When they are frightened, guinea pigs produce a slower, less excited whistle. Or they may grind their teeth or make a small "peep" sound when anxious.

▽ In Peru, guinea pigs are kept for food by the Quechua Indians. Like farmyard animals, they live in outhouses and backyards. They sometimes have the run of the dwellings themselves. Guinea pigs were domesticated and bred by the Inca Indians of Peru hundreds of years ago.

Keeping guinea pigs

It is best to buy young guinea pigs at 6 to 8 weeks old. At that age they are easy to tame. Because they are timid creatures, it is easier to make friends with guinea pigs when they are young.

Whether kept outdoors or indoors, guinea pigs should have a warm home, free from drafts. The floor of their cage may be covered with wood shavings, and their separate sleeping area with hay.

△ Always support a guinea pig from underneath when holding it, making sure that it cannot fall. But do not squeeze it.

Guinea pigs eat only vegetable food. They should be fed regularly with dry grain, greens, hay, seeds and nuts. A supply of clean water should be available at all times. Specially prepared pelleted food containing Vitamin C may be obtained from pet shops.

It is wise to have any ailments treated by a vet as soon as possible. Guinea pigs may fret, turning a simple disorder into a fatal one.

△ A mother and her young on the vet's table. Guinea pigs sometimes suffer from skin problems or upset stomachs, which need immediate treatment. They also might need their teeth cut down if they have grown too long.

Short-haired guinea pigs need little grooming. They keep themselves clean with their front paws. But their coat might need brushing to remove loose hairs. Long-haired guinea pigs need much more care.

Grooming a guinea pig for a show calls for attention to detail, such as removing all dead hairs. If gently handled, a guinea pig will soon get used to a bath in warm water and having its coat washed in a medicated baby shampoo.

▽ To keep an exhibition Peruvian's long coat clean, it must be put in wrappers. These keep it free from dirt and sawdust, and are removed only when grooming it or for a show. Preparing a long-haired guinea pig for the judges' table is like entering it in a beauty competition.

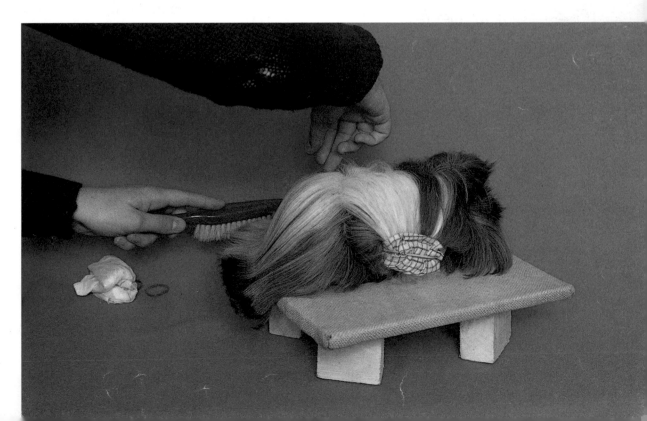

The story of guinea pigs

Discovering guinea pigs

The direct ancestors of the guinea pigs of today first appeared on earth about 20 million years ago. They were unknown to people of the Old World until the arrival in South America of the Spanish conquerors in the 1500s. The Spaniards found that guinea pigs had been kept as domestic animals by the Indians of Peru, Colombia and Ecuador for a long time. Remains of guinea pigs have been found in the tombs of the Incas, the original inhabitants of Peru. The Incas not only raised guinea pigs, but they also bred them with coats of different colors.

△ A stuffed Peruvian guinea pig of 1880 (top) compared with a modern slate-colored Peruvian.

Guinea pigs as food

The South American Indians kept guinea pigs for their meat, and lived closely with them. A Swiss explorer called Tschudi, who visited Peru in the 1800s, found guinea pigs living in the Indians' huts, and running all over the sleeping inhabitants at night. Guinea pigs are still eaten in large quantities in South America.

Introduction to Europe

Spanish explorers brought guinea pigs home with them. Records of 1564 refer to a little animal called the "Indian Hare or Piglet," which must have been one of the first guinea pigs to be seen in Europe. Guinea pigs became very popular. Fashionable ladies and gentlemen sometimes even had their pet guinea pigs painted alongside them in their portraits.

Guinea pigs and science

The guinea pig has for a long time been used in scientific research. It is an ideal laboratory animal, being easy to breed and tame. Its use in this way has passed into our language – we refer to anyone used for testing something out as a "guinea pig."

The white English Self breed is

△ Scientists of the early 1900s using guinea pigs in laboratory experiments.

the type most commonly used in laboratory work.

One of the guinea pig's most important contributions to research is in the study of Vitamin C deficiency, because, like us, the guinea pig is unable to make its own supply of this vitamin.

Showing

As more and more people began to raise guinea pigs, local groups were formed, and then national clubs to promote scientific breeding. The national organizations formulate show rules and the latest show standards – the points on which the guinea pigs are judged in competitions.

Breeders enter their prize guinea pigs in national and local shows. Most shows also have classes for junior or novice competitors – a good way to start showing your guinea pigs.

Facts and records

△ A religious painting of *The Last Supper*, which hangs in a cathedral in Peru. The dish in the center of the table contains … a large guinea pig! The painting was done by an artist of the 1500s or 1600s. But, of course, guinea pigs were not known in the Old World at the time of Christ.

Naming the guinea pig

No one knows for sure how the guinea pig got its name. It is not a pig, and it does not come from Guinea.

It may have been called after the Guineamen, seafarers who traded with Guinea, in Africa, but who also brought some of the first guinea pigs to Europe. Or possibly the name was confused with Guiana, an area of South America where some guinea pigs came from. The name may originally have been "coney" (rabbit) pig. Or perhaps they were sold for one guinea when they first arrived in England from overseas.

Guinea pig meat

In parts of South America guinea pigs are bred for size, fattened up for the table. Up to 60 million guinea pigs a year are eaten in Peru alone.

Glossary

Abyssinian
The rough-haired breed of guinea pig that has rosettes.

Agouti
Coloring in which the tip and root of each hair is of a different color from the part in between.

Boar
An adult male guinea pig.

Breed
A recognized type of domestic guinea pig. Each breed has its own special features and standards for showing.

Brindle
A coat color mixture of a dark and a light color.

Cavy or Cavia
Another name for the guinea pig, but also the name of the guinea pig family.

English
The name of the short-haired breeds of guinea pig.

Litter
The number of babies born at one time. Domestic guinea pig litters average three or four pups.

Peruvian
The main long-haired breed of guinea pig.

Pup
A baby guinea pig.

Rex
Another name for the Teddy breed.

Rosettes
The swirls that make up the coat of an Abyssinian guinea pig.

Self
Any guinea pig with a coat in one solid color.

Sheltie
A long-haired breed, also called Silkie.

Sow
An adult female guinea pig.

Species
A particular kind of animal òr plant. Animals of the same species breed young of that species.

Teddy
A rough-haired breed without rosettes.

Index